RAILWAYS IN LANCASHIRE

A Pictorial History

compiled by David Joy

DALESMAN BOOKS
1975

£1.25

The Dalesman Publishing Company Ltd.
Clapham (via Lancaster), North Yorkshire

First published 1975

© Text 1975 David Joy

ISBN: 0 85206 261 3

Printed in Great Britain by
Galava Printing Co. Ltd., Hallam Road, Nelson, Lancashire

Contents

The front cover shows "Clan" Pacific No. 72000 **Clan Buchanan** departing from Lancaster Castle with an up express. The back cover picture is of a Class 85 electric locomotive passing Warrington Bank Quay on a test train. Maps are by E. Gower.

Introduction

Lancashire—for good or ill—owes much of its present day character to the railway age. At the dawn of this age in 1830 the Liverpool & Manchester Railway "showed the world what could be done, and led to the greatest change in the habits of mankind that has ever come about otherwise than by a process of slow and gradual evolution". The dense network of lines which quickly grew up in south and central Lancashire made cotton king, so that by the middle of the 19th century it represented almost a third of the nation's trade. Manchester became the commercial hub of the industry and Liverpool its major port, the railways conveying both raw cotton inland and finished goods for export. Workers shuttled between home and mill on the hard horse-hair or wooden seats of third-class carriages, while the mill-owners commuted to and from the new residential areas in the plush comforts of first-class or even exclusive club cars.

The achievements of the railways were not, however, confined solely to the cotton trade. They opened up the south Lancashire coalfield and created the new port of Fleetwood, from where enormous quantities of fish were dispatched in special trains. They established locomotive works at Gorton and Horwich, which generated their own urban communities. And they were the prime influence in the spectacular growth of the seaside resorts of Morecambe, Southport and, especially, Blackpool—"seven golden miles" for the hundreds of thousands who flocked in by train from urban Lancashire.

This pictorial history embraces the pre-1974 boundaries of the county, but excluding Furness which is covered in the companion volume **Railways of the Lake Counties.** As was stated in the introduction to this work, "it is not just a collection of views, but an attempt to portray the character and customs, the pride and prejudice and the architectural attributes and atrocities of the region's various lines in their prime. Photographs taken from the same viewpoint during different decades show how fast the scene can change, and how a feature taken for granted can almost overnight become but a memory".

It would be impossible in a single volume to give comprehensive coverage of Lancashire, and the photographs necessarily select items of particular significance within the overall theme. Sketch maps on pages 6 and 7 show the principal lines but do not attempt to be comprehensive. Historical notes give a concise summary of each area's development, but for fuller information one should refer to the following selected list of further reading:

Bardsley, J. R., **The Railways of Bolton 1824-1959** (Author, 1960).

Box, C. E., **The Liverpool Overhead Railway 1893-1956** (Railway World, 1959).

Carlson, Robert E., **The Liverpool & Manchester Railway Project 1821-1831** (David & Charles, 1969).

Cook, R. A., **Lancashire & Yorkshire Railway Historical Maps** (Railway & Canal Historical Society, 1974).

Donaghy, Thomas J., **Liverpool & Manchester Railway Operations 1831-1845** (David & Charles, 1972).

Dow, George, **Great Central** (Locomotive Publishing Co., 3 vols., 1959-65).

Greville, M. D., **Chronology of the Railways of Lancashire** (Railway & Canal Historical Society, 1973).

Greville, M. D., & Holt, G. O., **The Lancaster & Preston Junction Railway** (David & Charles, 1961).

Griffiths, R. P., **The Cheshire Lines Railway** (Oakwood Press, 2nd edit., 1958).

Kellett, John R., **The Impact of Railways on Victorian Cities** (Routledge & Kegan Paul, 1969). (Chap. VI "Manchester"; Chap. VII "Liverpool").

Marshall, John, **The Lancashire & Yorkshire Railway** (David & Charles, 3 vols., 1969-72).

Nock, O. S., **The London & North Western Railway** (Ian Allan, 1960).

Norton, Peter, **Waterways and Railways to Warrington** (Railway & Canal Historical Society, 1974).

Parker, Norman, **The Preston & Longridge Railway** (Oakwood Press, 1972).

Reed, Brian, **Crewe to Carlisle** (Ian Allan, 1969).

Roberts, B., **Railways and Mineral Tramways of Rossendale** (Oakwood Press, 1974).

Rush, R. W., & Price, M. R., **The Garstang & Knott End Railway** (Oakwood Press, 1964).

Singleton, David, **Liverpool & Manchester Railway** (Dalesman Books, 1975).

Tattersall, W. D., **The Bolton, Blackburn, Clitheroe & West Yorkshire Railway** (Oakwood Press, 1973).

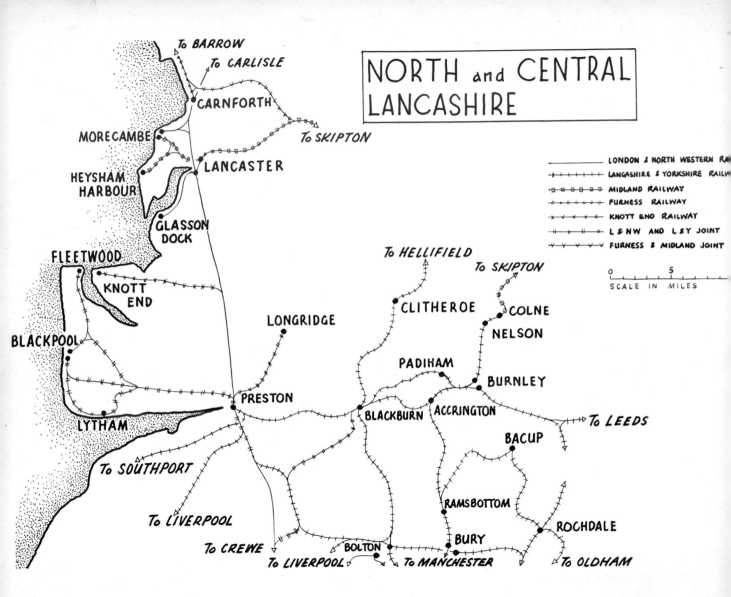

NORTH and CENTRAL LANCASHIRE

To BARROW
To CARLISLE
CARNFORTH
To SKIPTON
MORECAMBE
LANCASTER
HEYSHAM HARBOUR
GLASSON DOCK
FLEETWOOD
KNOTT END
BLACKPOOL
LYTHAM
LONGRIDGE
To HELLIFIELD
To SKIPTON
CLITHEROE
COLNE
NELSON
PADIHAM
BURNLEY
PRESTON
BLACKBURN
ACCRINGTON
To LEEDS
BACUP
To SOUTHPORT
RAMSBOTTOM
ROCHDALE
To LIVERPOOL
BURY
To OLDHAM
To CREWE
BOLTON
To LIVERPOOL
To MANCHESTER

LONDON & NORTH WESTERN RA—
LANCASHIRE & YORKSHIRE RAILW—
MIDLAND RAILWAY
FURNESS RAILWAY
KNOTT END RAILWAY
L & NW AND L & Y JOINT
FURNESS & MIDLAND JOINT

0   5
SCALE IN MILES

6

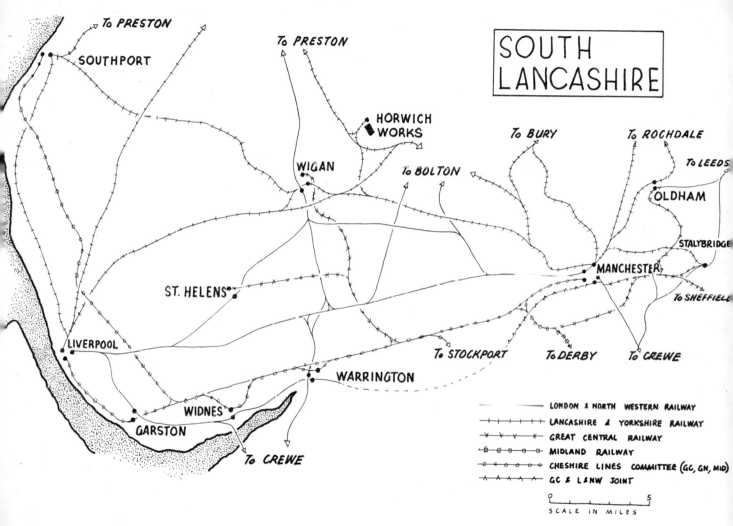

SOUTH LANCASHIRE

To PRESTON
SOUTHPORT
To PRESTON
HORWICH WORKS
To BURY
To ROCHDALE
To LEEDS
WIGAN
To BOLTON
OLDHAM
STALYBRIDGE
MANCHESTER
ST. HELENS
To SHEFFIELD
LIVERPOOL
To STOCKPORT
To DERBY
To CREWE
WARRINGTON
WIDNES
GARSTON
To CREWE

LONDON & NORTH WESTERN RAILWAY
LANCASHIRE & YORKSHIRE RAILWAY
GREAT CENTRAL RAILWAY
MIDLAND RAILWAY
CHESHIRE LINES COMMITTEE (GC, GN, MID)
GC & LNW JOINT

0   5
SCALE IN MILES

E GOWER

7

Merseyside and Southport

Merseyside, now a metropolitan county in its own right, has always had a totally different character to the rest of Lancashire. Much of this individual flavour stems from Liverpool's existence as a major port long before the dawn of the railway age. By the mid-1820's the town had a population of 135,000, was handling 10,000 ships a year and transporting a daily total of 1,000 tons of goods to and from Manchester. Hence there was a clear justification for the opening in 1830 of the Liverpool & Manchester Railway, the first "modern" railway in the world in that it carried both passengers and freight by locomotive haulage. Its initial passenger terminus at Crown Street, well outside the town centre, quickly proved inadequate and a new terminus at Lime Street was opened in 1836. Indicative of the times was the contribution of £2,000 by Liverpool Corporation towards the cost of enhancing the station façade. Trains from London (Euston Square) and Birmingham commenced to run through to Lime Street via Earlestown in 1837, a route that was followed until as late as 1869 when the high-level bridge over the Mersey at Runcorn was completed.

It was not until after the Liverpool & Manchester had become a constituent of the London & North Western Railway in 1846 that additional lines entered Liverpool. The Lancashire & Yorkshire Railway from Bury and its arch-rival, the East Lancashire Railway from Preston, somehow managed to share a common terminus at Great Howard Street from 1849. They moved to Tithebarn Street (later known as Exchange) the following year, but the feuding continued until the two companies amalgamated in 1859. Another important line into Exchange was the Liverpool, Crosby & Southport Railway, which was completed in 1850, absorbed by the L & Y in 1855 and electrified in 1904.

Liverpool's third major terminus—Central with its fine arched roof—was opened in 1874, replacing an earlier terminal at Brunswick Dock. It brought three further companies into the city as it was owned by the Cheshire Lines Committee which comprised the Manchester, Sheffield & Lincolnshire (later Great Central), Great Northern and Midland railways. In 1879 the CLC opened a line through the eastern suburbs of Liverpool from Hunt's Cross to Aintree and extended it to Southport five years later.

A railway occupying a unique place in the life of Liverpool was not completed until 1896. The Liverpool Overhead Railway, extending from Dingle to Seaforth Sands, was the first electric line in the city, the first elevated electric railway in the world and the first to use an automatic signalling system. Diametrically opposed to it was the Mersey Railway, which came under the river from Birkenhead to a terminus beneath Central Station. Steamworked from opening in 1886, the "foul fumes" of its locomotives were displaced by electric traction in 1903.

A 1914 interior view of Lime Street, best-known of the Liverpool termini. Opened in 1836 as a replacement for the Liverpool & Manchester Railway's Crown Street terminus, it was rebuilt in 1846-51 and again in 1868-71.

By 1964 the architectural features of the station were almost lost above the cat's cradle of overhead wires which marked the onset of 25kv electrification. Many services are, however, still diesel-hauled, as instanced here by D280 about to depart with an up express.

Among the finest photographs of the steam locomotive scene are those taken by Eric Treacy around Lime Street and Edge Hill. Four of them appear on this and the next three pages.

Both of these views are at the same location at Edge Hill. Opposite is unrebuilt "Scot" 6127 **Old Contemptibles.** Above is 6225 **Duchess of Gloucester** in its original streamlined condition on the up Red Rose express.

Rebuilt "Patriot" 45521 **Rhyl** pounds through the Lime Street cutting with the up Merseyside Express.

"Jubilee" 45704 **Leviathan** adds to the already smoky atmosphere as it departs from Lime Street in pre-electrification days.

A striking illustration of the decline and fall of the Moorish Arch at Edge Hill, the point where locomotive-working on the Liverpool & Manchester Railway gave way to cable haulage for the journey into the Crown Street terminus. The above print shows the scene shortly after opening in 1830.

Almost a century-and-a-half later a photograph from an identical viewpoint shows that the Arch has completely vanished but several features on the cutting walls still remain. Note particularly the steps and the arches beneath them.

Olive Mount cutting, originally just two tracks wide, must have been an awe-inspiring spectacle to the first travellers on the Liverpool & Manchester Railway. Over 80 feet deep and almost two miles long, it is noted for its sheer rock walls. This view dates from 1946.

Railways—and photography— were still in their pioneering stage when this cableless Allan 2-2-2 and a train of box-like coaches posed for the camera about 1865. The location is Broad Green, first station east of Edge Hill on the Liverpool & Manchester Railway.

Webb 0-6-2 tank No. 7751 at Garston Dock on the 5-13 p.m. for Liverpool Lime Street on 12th June, 1947. This now forgotten passenger service was withdrawn four days later.

Trains from Lime Street to London ceased to travel via the Liverpool & Manchester Railway and Earlestown in 1869 when the cut-off over the Mersey at Runcorn was opened. The impressive viaduct here is 75 feet above high water and each of the three spans is 305 feet long.

Other Liverpool termini were not as well-known as Lime Street but had equally noteworthy approaches. Wapping, the original freight terminus of the Liverpool & Manchester Railway, was reached by a tunnel over $1\frac{1}{4}$ miles long through which wagons were lowered by cable. This is a view from the western end of the main tunnel, just after closure in 1965, showing the short subsidiary tunnels into the goods depot.

The unpretentious Riverside terminus was opened in 1895 when trans-Atlantic steamer travel was at its height, and was used by boat expresses which completed their journey with a tortuous passage over the lines of the Mersey Dock & Harbour Board. With the decline in this type of traffic it has now closed. The view here dates from 1914.

A unique Merseyside institution was the Liverpool Overhead Railway, at the time of its opening in 1893 the first overhead electric railway in the world. Extending for $6\frac{1}{4}$ miles along the city's waterfront, it was known throughout Liverpool as the "Dockers' Umbrella". Here a train is leaving Pier Head station in 1950.

By 1956 the decking of the Overhead Railway required renewal at a cost of £2 million, and neither the company nor the Corporation were prepared to meet the bill. Unfortunately for Liverpool's future transport needs, a line carrying ten million passengers a year was therefore closed and dismantled.

Liverpool Central was the terminus not of a single railway but of the Cheshire Lines Committee. This comprised the Great Central, Great Northern and Midland railways, and in fact had the greater part of its mileage in Lancashire! In this 1950 scene ex-Great Central 0-6-2T No. 69337 is station pilot.

In pre-Grouping days Great Central 4-4-0 No. 875 heads a CLC Liverpool-Manchester express through Hunts Cross, east of Garston.

The main CLC shed for Liverpool was at Brunswick, and in this delightful pre-Grouping view it boasts a fine array of Great Central locomotives. Note also the magnificent lamp.

By 1950 only the shell of the shed remained, but the motive power was still largely ex-Great Central. The lamp alas had been replaced by a utilitarian electric fitting on top of a pole.

The Lancashire & Yorkshire Railway's Liverpool terminus was Exchange with its high-pitched roof and broad cab drive seen in the centre of this 1964 view. The station dates from 1884-8, when it replaced an earlier structure originally known as Tithebarn Street and opened in 1850.

It was the summer of 1902 when Lancashire & Yorkshire 4-4-0 No. 890 posed on the turntable outside Liverpool Exchange.

Another Merseyside institution is Aintree racecourse, where the Lancashire & Yorkshire Railway built a special station. On Grand National Day, 1930, ex-London & North Western Railway 4-6-0 No. 5776 discharges its packed train of race-goers.

In the heyday of the railway there was much residential and holiday traffic between Liverpool and Southport. This fine period study in a Southport train is believed to have been taken on the CLC route.

The CLC terminus at Southport Lord Street in 1948, with ex-Great Central 4-4-0 No. 6019 on a Warrington train. The CLC provided the best route from Southport to Widnes and Warrington, but not to Liverpool or Manchester.

The Lancashire & Yorkshire line from Liverpool Exchange to Southport Chapel Street was electrified in 1904 when this photograph was taken at Formby. An intensive service of 75 trains each day was introduced, station times being cut to a minimum by the platform boards telling passengers where to stand.

Unconventional motive power
at Southport Chapel Street in
1923 in the form of the
Ramsay-Wier turbine
locomotive. It worked mainly
in the Bolton area, and was
never taken into railway
ownership.

More familiar but still novel in
concept was the Sentinel
steam railcar, which was used
widely on lightly-loaded
services in the 1920s and '30s.
Here a CLC railcar pauses
between duties at Southport
Lord Street.

South Lancashire

The railways of south Lancashire at first sight seem to form a bewildering maze around the towns of St. Helens, Warrington, Widnes and Wigan, but basically they comprise one north-south main line, four routes between Liverpool and Manchester and numerous connecting links. Key locations on the Liverpool & Manchester Railway in this region during much of the 19th century were Newton Junction (later known as Earlestown) and Parkside a few miles to the east. The former was the divergence point for the Warrington & Newton Railway, opened in 1831 but of purely local significance until 1837 when it became part of the Grand Junction Railway from Birmingham and a new through station was opened at Warrington. From this date trains from London (Euston) came north to Newton Junction, from where some would head westwards to Liverpool.

Others turned eastwards to Parkside, thence to continue to Manchester or alternatively again travel north over the Wigan Branch Railway. This had been opened in 1832 and two years later absorbed by the North Union Railway, which in 1838 completed a new through station at Wigan and an extension to Preston. All these lines except the North Union (see "Preston and the Fylde") became part of the London & North Western Railway in 1846, but it was not until 1864 that a cut-off was opened and West Coast route traffic ceased to use a short stretch of the Liverpool & Manchester. Further decline of this railway cross-roads came during the same year when L & NW traffic from Manchester to the north began to take the new Eccles - Wigan direct line. Similarly, a Huyton - St.

Helens - Wigan link completed five years later carried trains from Liverpool to the north which had previously travelled via Parkside.

The second route from Liverpool to Manchester was completed in 1848 by the L & Y's Liverpool-Bolton-Bury railway which joined the earlier Manchester-Bolton-Preston line at Lostock Junction. Its original station at Wigan, described as "a hovel", became the junction for a direct line to Southport in 1855. An important cut-off through Atherton enabling L & Y expresses from Manchester to Preston and Wigan to avoid Bolton was opened in 1888.

The third Liverpool-Manchester route grew out of the St. Helens Railway which opened in 1832 from St. Helens to Widnes (then Runcorn Gap), from where it had extended west to Garston and east to Warrington by 1853. The following year a through link to Altrincham, and hence Manchester, was created by the Warrington & Stockport Railway. Both of these companies had become part of the L & NW by 1864, but the route as a whole was eclipsed by the fourth and more direct link between the two cities which was created by the opening of the main line of the Cheshire Lines Committee in 1873. It served Warrington and Widnes by means of loops, the latter being built solely by the Manchester, Sheffield & Lincolnshire and Midland railways. A branch from the CLC at Glazebrook became wholly Great Central when in 1906 the company took over independent lines which had given St. Helens a second station and Wigan a third in terminating at these two towns.

The West Coast main line in bygone days. Standish, north of Wigan, about 1900, with an 0-8-0 goods locomotive heading north.

Wigan station, now totally transformed with the onset of electrification. A "Prince of Wales" class 4-6-0 No. 1123 pauses on an up semi-fast.

One of the best-known features on the central section of the Liverpool & Manchester Railway is the skew bridge at Rainhill, probably the first of this size to be built over a railway at an angle. It cost £3,735, quite a substantial sum for those days. This engraving is contemporary with the opening of the line.

Today the bridge remains basically unchanged, although one of the station platforms runs up to it. On the platform is an enamelled plaque commemorating the famous Rainhill trials of 1829 which were won by Robert Stephenson's **Rocket** (not George Stephenson's as erroneously stated on the plaque!).

A fascinating early engraving of the North Union Railway bridge at Wigan, taking the West Coast main line over the Lancashire & Yorkshire's Liverpool-Bury route. The lines were opened respectively in 1838 and 1848.

Class 5MT 4-6-0 No. 45296 passing under the same bridge in 1967. Development has obstructed the view of the church, but otherwise the scene has altered little.

Horwich, at the end of a branch line, was at first sight a strange place for the Lancashire & Yorkshire's locomotive works, but land happened to be available here when the company required new premises in the 1880s. These views show: (above) three of the fleet of 18 in. gauge works shunters; (top right) the erecting shop in 1961; (bottom right) rail-motor at Horwich station on the branch passenger service.

Industrial south Lancashire had a surprising number of secondary lines and services which epitomised the inefficiences of the traditional steam railway. In this 1951 view there are five staff but no passengers at Sutton Oak, served until 1964 by a shuttle service between St. Helens and St. Helens Junction on the Liverpool & Manchester Railway.

Another way of approaching the glass-making town was via the former Great Central branch which left the CLC main line at Glazebrook and ultimately terminated at St. Helen's Central—the most rudimentary of termini. Ex-GC 0-6-0 No. 65189 prepares to run round its train in 1951.

The London & North Western station at Walkden on the line from Manchester Exchange to Bolton Great Moor Street seems to have been a favourite with early photographers. This view looking towards Manchester dates from LMS days, but the locomotive and station are still very much North Western.

A pre-Grouping view looking towards Bolton. The higher bridge in the background carries the Lancashire & Yorkshire main line from Manchester Victoria to Liverpool, Southport and Preston.

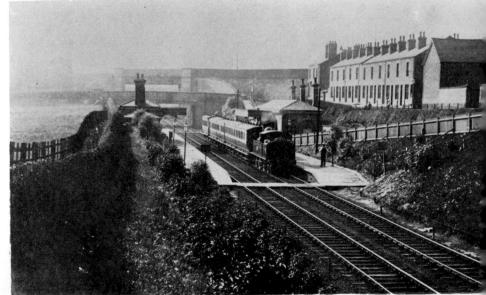

Another pre-Grouping scene, with quite a cluster of passengers on the platform. The station was approached by no less than four sloping footways.

The scene today from the same viewpoint as the photograph opposite. Following closure the line has been landscaped and turned into a useful and attractive footpath.

Numerous industrial lines dotted the landscape of south Lancashire. The Walkden Colliery lines were among the most visited because of their ex-North Staffordshire Railway 0-6-2 tanks. **Princess,** seen here in 1951, has now been preserved in North Staffordshire livery.

Photographs of colliers' trains are rare, which makes this view of a Bridgewater Collieries' train at Ashton Field of particular interest. The locomotive is Manning Wardle 0-6-0 saddle-tank No. 311 of 1870, and is named **Francis.**

A superb study of Lancashire & Yorkshire 4-4-2 No. 1422 on Walkden troughs with a Manchester-Blackpool express.

Around Manchester

The early railways into Manchester stopped well outside the city centre, and until 1844 there were quite simply four unconnected termini. The first in the field was the Liverpool & Manchester Railway's Liverpool Road station of 1830, which from 1837 also became the departure point for London with the completion of the Grand Junction Railway. In 1838 the Manchester, Bolton & Bury Canal Navigation & Railway opened a line running from Salford alongside the earlier canal to Bolton. A year later the first section of the Manchester & Leeds Railway from a terminal at Oldham Road to Littleborough was brought into use; it reached Leeds in 1841 with the completion of the great Summit tunnel. Finally, in 1840 the Manchester & Birmingham Railway opened as far as Stockport from a temporary terminus at Travis Street, shared from the following year by trains using the completed portion of the Sheffield, Ashton-under-Lyne & Manchester Railway as far as Guide Bridge. A permanent station at London Road was opened in 1842, when extension beyond Stockport to Crewe created a more direct route to the south.

A major attempt at unification in 1844 saw the Manchester & Leeds extending to a new central station at Victoria, to which the Liverpool & Manchester built a link through Salford where there was a connection with the Bolton line. By 1847 the M & L and the Bolton company had become part of the new Lancashire & Yorkshire Railway, while the L & M was a constituent of the London & North Western Railway, so that Victoria station formed uneasy common ground between these two major companies. Matters were made worse from 1849 when the L & NW started to run over the L & Y Stalybridge line in order to gain access to its direct route to Leeds via Standedge tunnel and Huddersfield. It was not until 1884 that the L & NW finally built its own separate station at Exchange.

The situation became much more inflamed on the south side of the city after the Sheffield company had completed its route through Woodhead tunnel and had become part of the Manchester, Sheffield & Lincolnshire Railway in 1847. Its neighbour at London Road was now a constituent of the L & NW, which tried in every way to intimidate the MS & L: "Signs were painted out, members of the public misdirected or even taken into custody for using the wrong platforms or tickets, ticket clerks forcibly ejected through the booking office windows, a pitched battle took place for the physical possession of a shed." Harmony was eventually restored, and from 1899 London Road was a common departure point for Great Central (formerly MS & L) expresses to London (Marylebone) and those of the L & NW to Euston.

A third London-Manchester route was created in 1867 when Midland trains from Derby commenced to run through the Peak District and into London Road, at first via Hyde and then via Reddish. They were diverted to Central in 1880, when the last of Manchester's major termini was completed by the Cheshire Lines Committee.

Manchester (Liverpool Road), the original terminus of the Liverpool & Manchester Railway and now the oldest railway station in the world. Note the rail-level platform. Plans for making it the basis of a transport museum were announced in 1974.

Passenger trains ceased to use Liverpool Road in 1844 when they were transfered to the new Victoria station, which also handled the traffic of the Manchester & Leeds Railway. This lithograph by A. F. Tait shows on the right two of the composite coaches known as "Gondolas"—the first-class was covered and the second-class open.

Hughes 4-6-0 No. 1507 departs from Manchester Victoria with a Newcastle-Liverpool express made up of North Eastern Railway coaching stock. On the extreme left Midland Railway 4-4-0 No. 591 is heading one of the Manchester-Hellifield trains which the company worked in conjunction with its Anglo-Scottish expresses.

An early view, thought to be of the north side of Victoria. The presence of "DX" class 0-6-0 No. 1080 on a London & North Western train indicates that the photograph was taken prior to 1884 when the company began to use its new Exchange station.

A Lancashire & Yorkshire 4-4-0 briskly accelerates out of Victoria with a westbound express. It is passing "the back" of Exchange, a station which in effect formed relief platforms for Victoria and has now closed.

5MT 4-6-0 No. 5402 at Exchange in 1946. The "Lavatory for Gentlemen" sign is a fine example of railway phraseology.

The changing façade of Exchange station. Tramcars and early taxi-cabs were the only users of the road about 1920 when the railways were still wallowing in complacent maturity.

Today the scene is car-orientated, and even the statue has had to be moved in the name of progress. The closed Exchange station has lost its frontage, and the approach has become a car park.

The Lancashire & Yorkshire's main locomotive shed for Manchester, and the largest on its system, was Newton Heath. It had 24 stabling roads and an allocation of some 200 locomotives, just a few of which are visible in this view of 25th August, 1921.

The scope and complexity of workings from Newton Heath is shown by the engine arrangements board on the same date. As it is an August Saturday, there are numerous special workings to Blackpool, Fleetwood, Llandudno and Scarborough.

Manchester London Road (now Piccadilly) was in effect two termini in one—London & North Western services from Euston and Crewe used one side, and Great Central trains from Marylebone and Sheffield the other. Here L & NW "Alfred the Great" class 4-4-0 No. 1950 **Victorious** is departing with an up express.

The North Staffordshire Railway worked over the L & NW into London Road from the northern extremity of its own system at Macclesfield. Immaculately groomed 0-6-0 No. 120 awaits the "right-away", as does a Great Central tank on the other side of the fence separating the two halves of the station.

4MT 2-6-4T No. 42399 pilots "Jubilee" 45624 **St. Helena** out of London Road with a Euston express. On the right is one of the Bo + Bos built for the Manchester-Sheffield electrification scheme of 1954.

43

To ease congestion at London Road, a separate terminus known as Manchester Mayfield was opened in 1910. Until its closure in 1960 it handled mainly local trains, like the one shown here in 1946 headed by 2-6-4T No. 2318.

A typical steam-age suburban train pauses at Gorton & Openshaw on the Great Central line out of London Road. The locomotive is ex-GC 4-4-2 tank No. 7423.

A few miles east of Gorton is Guide Bridge, a favourite location with photographers. In LNER days ex-Great Central 4-4-0 No. 5505 heads an express past a coal train sporting a good example of a private owner's wagon.

Until 1897 the Great Central Railway was the more provincial Manchester, Sheffield & Lincolnshire Railway, and therefore the Manchester area was a natural location for its Gorton locomotive works. Opened in 1848, it was still a hive of activity when this view was taken in pre-war days but closed in the 1960s.

The Cheshire Lines Committee's Manchester Central terminus opened in 1880, and won critical acclaim for its magnificent arched roof with an uninterrupted span of 210 feet. All was peace and tranquility when this view was taken just a few weeks before closure on 5th May, 1969.

The terminus has indeed fallen on hard times by being used as a car park, but a more worthy fate may be in store. Plans have been announced to use the train shed as an exhibition hall.

In the golden age of the railways, a spotless Great Central 4-4-0 No. 440 awaits departure from Manchester Central.

An ex-GC 4-6-2 tank No. 69805 on express duties in 1955. It is heading a Liverpool Central-Hull train through Fallowfield on the connecting link from the CLC to the Great Central main line. The tank would be replaced at Guide Bridge by an electric locomotive for the climb over the Pennines through Woodhead tunnel.

Characteristic of suburban stations on the west side of Manchester was Monton Green, seen here about 1910. It was the first station on the London & North Western route to Wigan after leaving the Liverpool & Manchester Railway.

Not far to the east was the even more disreputable Irlams-o'-th'-Height on the parallel Lancashire & Yorkshire route. L & NW "Claughton" class 4-6-0 No. 192 shows the L & Y a thing or two by pounding through the station with a vast Manchester-Blackpool test train in 1922, the year in which the two companies amalgamated in advance of the Grouping.

Urmston, on the CLC main line, has always had a heavy commuter traffic. In this scene around the turn of the century passengers are protected from the rain as they await a Manchester-bound train. If it was late they at least had plenty of advertisements to read.

Today the canopy and most of the advertisements have vanished. The station is, however, very adequately lit.

The affinity between the interior of Werneth station and that of a chapel of the same period is quite unmistakable. Until 1847, when the line was extended, the station was the terminus for Oldham.

The original approach to Werneth was the famous and initially rope-worked 1 in 27 incline from Middleton Junction on the Manchester & Leeds Railway. Its gradient can clearly be seen in this view from the station platform; on the left—and descending at 1 in 50—is the later line of 1880 through Hollinwood. The Werneth incline closed in 1963.

Saddleworth, on the London & North Western route through the Pennines from Manchester to Leeds, only came into Lancashire in 1974 but geographically was always very much part of the county. A Manchester-bound train is crossing Saddleworth viaduct; on the left is the short branch to Delph.

Like something out of a film comedy, the Lancashire & Yorkshire's fire train rushes past Middleton Junction on a "call-out". The rolling stock comprises a Shand-Mason steam fire pump on a dropside wagon, a large water tank and a four-wheeled coach !

East Lancashire

The East Lancashire Railway, among the most colourful of the early companies in the county, had as its most important section a main line extending from Clifton Junction through Bury to Accrington which was completed in 1848. The company absorbed several railways, so that Accrington was on the one hand the junction of a line from Liverpool, Preston and Blackburn, and on the other the start of an extension to Burnley, Nelson and Colne. All these routes were in operation by 1850. At Colne an end-on junction was made with the Leeds & Bradford Railway (later the Midland) from Skipton, and for a brief period in 1849 through Leeds-Liverpool trains came this way in competition with those of the rival Lancashire & Yorkshire Railway.

The most famous result of the conflict between these two companies was the "Battle of Clifton Junction" on March 12th, 1849, when the L & Y attempted to stop East Lancashire trains proceeding over its metals into Manchester. A baulk of timber placed across the rails by the L & Y was removed by the EL, so as a next step trains of the rival companies engaged in a "push-of-war" which proved inconclusive. Reinforcements in the form of additional trains were brought in by both parties, and the contest culminated in no less than eight trains being snarled up at the junction.

The East Lancashire Railway finally amalgamated with the L & Y in 1859, but by this time its territory had already been penetrated by the Manchester company. Todmorden, just inside Yorkshire and reached by the Manchester & Leeds main line through Summit tunnel, provided the jumping-off point for a picturesque route climbing through the Cliviger gorge and then descending to a separate station at Burnley Thorneybank (later Manchester Road). Opened in 1849, it came to be an important link from the West Riding to Preston and Blackpool. Another offshoot of the M & L was an 1841 horse-worked branch from Blue Pits, near Castleton, to Heywood. This soon became a locomotive-worked line and in 1848 was extended to a low-level station at Bury Knowsley Street, where it linked up with the Liverpool-Bury route.

Bacup, an upland cotton town in the narrow confines of the Rossendale valley, became the terminus in 1852 for an East Lancashire branch from Stubbins via Rawtenstall. In 1870 the L & Y opened a branch from Rochdale to serve stone quarries at Facit, and eleven years later this was extended northwards to provide an alternative approach to Bacup.

A. F. Tait's engraving of Rochdale station gives an excellent impression of main line passenger facilities in the mid-1840s. Note particularly the covered waiting area on the left set back a considerable distance from the rails; also the engine shed in the right background with its tall chimney.

A portion of the original Manchester & Leeds Railway buildings at Rochdale still survives and is used by the district engineer.

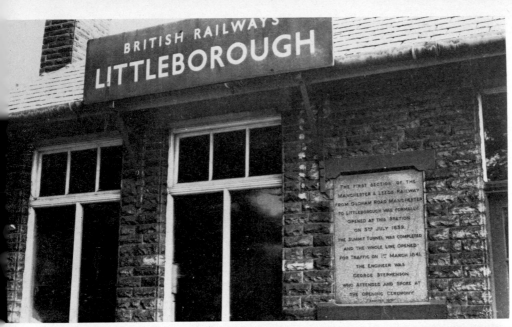

A plaque at Littleborough commemorates the opening of the first section of the Manchester & Leeds Railway on 3rd July, 1839. The fares for the 13½ miles were a then expensive 4s first class, 2s 6d second class and 1s 6d third class.

The major work on the Manchester & Leeds was Summit tunnel, which cost £251,000 and consumed 23 million bricks. At 1 mile 1,125 yards it was the longest in the world at the time of its completion in 1841. This view is looking out of the east end through the short Summit East tunnel to Deanroyd tunnel.

The line from Rochdale to Facit and Bacup was one of the most impressive in Lancashire, climbing on gradients as steep as 1 in 39 to a summit almost a thousand feet above sea level at Britannia. Its engineering works included the 105 feet high single-line Healey Dell viaduct, shown here about 1905 being crossed by a 2-4-2 tank and train.

Bacup, an upland cotton town once served by lines from both Ramsbottom and Rochdale, still had a busy four-road engine shed in 1937. It looked very much as if it had been hewn out of the bleak moorlands surrounding the town.

A useful cross-country link is the steeply-graded and scenically spectacular line from Todmorden to Burnley, carrying heavy holiday traffic between the West Riding and Blackpool. At the Burnley end of the line a train passes Towneley station and its imposing signal box.

Beyond Burnley, Blackpool-bound trains next pass Rose Grove, shown in this early photograph with low-level platforms prior to rebuilding in 1897.

The most impressive portion of the Todmorden-Burnley line is just over the Yorkshire border where it emerges straight from the 290 yard Kitson Wood tunnel on to Nott Wood viaduct. "Britannia" class No. 70013 **Oliver Cromwell** is crossing with one of the "end-of-steam" specials in 1968.

Greenmount station on the Bury-Holcombe Brook branch. This had a chequered career, being opened by the independent Bury & Tottington District Railway in 1882, absorbed by the L & Y six years later, electrified on the overhead system in 1913 and then the third rail in 1917, reverting to steam haulage in 1951 and closing to passengers the following year.

Two locomotives bank a heavy freight up Baxenden incline which climbed more than 250 feet in less than two miles. It was just south of Accrington on the ex-East Lancashire Railway's Bury line.

A remarkable early photograph of 2-4-0 **Milo,** built for the L & Y in 1849 by Sharp Bros. of Atlas Works, Manchester. It was taken at Colne, and must therefore be dated between 1859 (when the L & Y began to work into the town) and 1863 (when the locomotive was rebuilt with a cab).

Equally remarkable in its own way is **Excelsior,** a traction engine on rails built by Aveling & Porter in 1880 for the isolated 3 ft. gauge Scout Moor tramway at Edenfield. It was withdrawn about 1910 and then left outside to rot for 50 years until it was removed for preservation in 1961 by Aveling Barford. The engine originally had a hinged chimney so that it could enter its shed !

Accrington was where the two main lines of the East Lancashire Railway — from Liverpool and Clifton Junction, near Manchester—joined before continuing to Colne. Set into the "V" of the junction it was once a very busy station with ample passenger facilities. It is seen here about 1910.

Today the direct line to Manchester is closed and Accrington has become a basic through station with minimal buildings but retaining what would appear to be the original footbridge.

It is often forgotten that Colne was once a joint station, shared betwen the L & Y and the Midland which entered Lancashire from Skipton. In 1965 it still possessed many Midland features and handled quite a variety of traffic.

Ten years later the station had been reduced to a pathetic "bus shelter" with a single line terminating at a buffer stop. The Colne-Skipton section was closed in 1970.

North from Bolton

Despite its many claims to fame, the Liverpool & Manchester was not the first public railway in Lancashire. This distinction belongs to the Bolton & Leigh Railway which opened for goods traffic two years earlier in 1828. Passengers were not, however, carried until 1831 when the opening of the Kenyon & Leigh Junction Railway created a direct route from Bolton to Liverpool via the L & M. The Bolton terminus became known as Great Moor Street, and from 1875 was also served by a direct London & North Western line from Manchester via Walkden.

Trinity Street, Bolton's other station, was also early in the field. It was the terminus for the 1838 Manchester, Bolton & Bury Canal Navigation and Railway, the oldest constituent of the L & Y, and ten years later had been reached by lines from Preston, Liverpool, Bury and Blackburn. The latter was completed in 1848 by the Bolton, Blackburn, Clitheroe & West Yorkshire Railway, which reached a terminus at Chatburn, north of Clitheroe, two years later. At Blackburn the company had its own station at Darwen Street, but was forced to share the tracks of the East Lancashire Railway's Accrington-Liverpool line for about three-quarters of a mile.

This led to another famous dispute at Daisy Hill junction on the Chatburn side of Blackburn. The company had refused to pay a heavy toll demanded by the East Lancashire for the use of its lines, so on the opening day the first train from Clitheroe arrived at the junction to find it blocked and some 200 navvies assembled with engines and a train of stone wagons. One train was allowed to pass on payment of the toll, but an attempt was then made to drop passengers off short of the junction so that they could finish their journey on foot while the empty train was taken past the East Lancashire officials ! The subterfuge failed, but a normal service commenced two days later. The Blackburn company was so harassed by its competitors that it was driven to an amalgamation jointly with the East Lancashire and L & Y in 1857.

Years later in 1879-80 the L & Y extended the line north from Chatburn to a junction with the Midland at Hellifield, thus establishing a new route from Lancashire to Scotland via the Settle-Carlisle railway. In 1888 the Midland took over the working of all Scottish traffic from Liverpool Exchange and Manchester Victoria via Hellifield, and in the following year began to work many of the Manchester-Bolton-Blackburn trains which included through coaches from St. Pancras. Blackburn also became an outpost of the London & North Western with the opening in 1869 of the Lancashire Union Railway (L & Y and L & NW Joint) from Boar's Head, north of Wigan, to Cherry Tree just west of Blackburn.

The major engineering work on the Bolton-Blackburn line is Sough tunnel, 1 mile 255 yards long. 4MT 2-6-4 tank No. 42303 is emerging into the deep cutting at the south end of the tunnel in 1960.

"Jubilee" class 4-6-0 No. 45679 **Armanda** passes 4F 0-6-0 No. 44363 as it leaves Bolton Trinity Street with a Fleetwood-Manchester train in 1961. The station was completely rebuilt in 1899-1904.

One of the directors of the 1845 Blackburn, Darwen & Bolton Railway was cotton baron James Kay of Turton Tower, who insisted that the road to his country seat be carried over the line by a large ornamental bridge. It still survives, and in this 1961 view is framing B1 No. 61298 hauling a Glasgow-Manchester goods.

A curious location for a signal box was that of Bolton Station Down, which looked most unsafe on its seemingly perilous perch above the tracks. The locomotive on the left is 4MT 2-6-4 tank No. 42565, and the date is May 1964.

Not in the Bolton/Blackburn area, but nevertheless equally remarkable was Ilex Hall Carr box on the Ramsbottom-Bacup line. It is possibly the only signal box ever built in a river!

Blackburn station about 1900, some twelve years after it had been rebuilt with an undistinguished overall roof but some very fine lamps and clocks.

The station has altered only slightly in the last seventy years. The platform on the left has been cut back and taken out of passenger use, but the clocks still remain.

Rishton station on the Blackburn-Accrington line, reminiscent of a farmstead with its passenger facilities, station master's house and goods shed all under a single roof. The architecture does, however, blend well with the surroundings.

Despite its urban bias, the Lancashire & Yorkshire made every effort to make the most of its few rural lines. This poster, with its pictures of Clitheroe Castle, the Ribble at Gisburn and Stonyhurst College, dates from about 1897.

A classic photograph of the original Clitheroe station before its replacement in 1869-70. The 0-6-0 locomotive No. 224, built at Miles Platting in 1854, has a conspicuous headlamp on which the code was varied by a variety of coloured lenses. The wagons belong to the Tawd Vale Coal Co., Skelmersdale.

A well-groomed Barton Wright 4-4-0 at the second Clitheroe station about 1886. By this time the former Blackburn, Clitheroe & North Western Junction Railway had been extended from Chatburn through to Hellifield, thus opening up a new route from Lancashire to Scotland.

The Clitheroe area once supplied large quantities of milk by rail to the Manchester area. In this scene from a bygone era farmers are waiting to deliver their churns at the station about 1900.

Clitheroe station in 1960, two years before the withdrawal of the Blackburn-Hellifield passenger service.

Preston and the Fylde

As the result of electrification Preston is now the most important stopping point on the West Coast main line, but it has always been the key railway centre of mid-Lancashire. The main line reached the town in 1838 in the form of the Wigan-Preston section of the North Union Railway, its terminus being on the same site as that of today's main line station. The next stage of the West Coast route was not north from Preston but westwards to Fleetwood, from where passengers took a steamer to Ardrossan for Glasgow. The town and port were created "from a rabbit warren" by Sir Peter Hesketh Fleetwood as an integral part of the Preston & Wyre Railway, which was worked by the North Union from its opening in 1840.

The same year saw the opening of the Lancaster & Preston Junction Railway, but it was not until completion of the Scottish section of the West Coast main line in 1848 that the Ardrossan steamers became obsolete. The L & PJ soon got at odds with the North Union, and for a time used the separate Maxwell House station of the 1843 Bolton & Preston Railway. However, this latter company was absorbed by the North Union in 1844 after an intensive rate war for Manchester traffic. All main line services into Preston, including those of the Preston & Wyre which had used a separate terminus at Maudlands, then ran into the North Union station.

The NU was jointly leased in 1846 by companies which became the Lancashire & Yorkshire and London & North Western railways, and in 1889 the lines from Bolton and Parkside to their common meeting point at Euxton were respectively transferred to the L & Y and L & NW. Similarly, the Preston & Wyre, which opened extensions to both Blackpool and Lytham in 1846, was jointly owned by the L & Y and L & NW from 1849.

East Lancashire Railway routes to Preston from Blackburn and Liverpool had their own portion of the NU station from 1850. Another company, the Preston & Longridge, initially had separate termini at Deepdale Street and then Maudlands Bridge, but after it too had become the joint property of the L & Y and L & NW its trains began to run into the main line station in 1885. Finally, the 1882 West Lancashire Railway from Southport had its own terminus at Fishergate Hill until absorption by the L & Y saw this being abandoned in 1900.

Prior to the introduction of dining cars in the 1890s, Preston was the refreshment stop for West Coast expresses and for many years a meal served by "a hot and perspiring woman" had to be gulped down in 20 minutes. Such scenes have now vanished beyond recall, as has the railway heyday of Blackpool when well over 300,000 passengers would converge on the resort's two termini in an August weekend.

Preston station, once described as "one of the most dismal, dilapidated, disgraceful-looking structures in Christendom", had by the time this view was taken about 1912 become the respectable hub of services in much of central Lancashire. Today, with electrification, it is the mid-point on the West Coast route and both London and Glasgow can be reached in little more than 2½ hours.

The East Lancashire section of Preston station, now swept away as part of modernisation, had its own entrance and was virtually self-contained. 4-4-0 No. 10129 is at the head of the Liverpool portion of the 10-20 a.m. ex Glasgow in September 1930.

Un-named "Patriot" class 4 6-0 No. 45544 passes the former Preston No. 1 signal box with a ~~Euston~~-Barrow express. *To Euston*

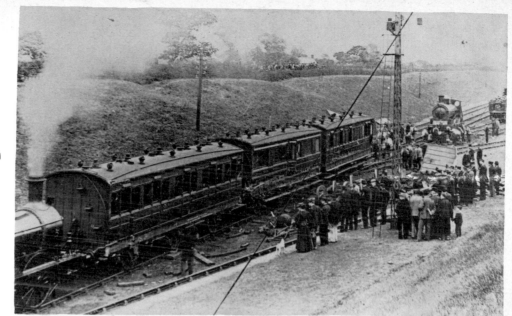

Aftermath of an accident at Preston junction on 3rd August, 1896. The culprit is in the background—having lost its tender in the process.

Modern signalling has done much to reduce the number of railway accidents. An amazing installation is the new Preston power box, which not only controls the electrified West Coast route to a point north of Carnforth but also lines extending as far east as Hebden Bridge—more than thirty miles away in West Yorkshire !

Heyday of steam on the West Coast route. "Precedent" class 2-4-0 No. 12 **Lazonby** pilots "Claughton" class 4-6-0 No. 2204 **Sir Herbert Walker, K.C.B.** on a fifteen-coach Carlisle-Euston express near Preston.

0 6 0 No. 8290 ambles along with a lightweight goods near Garstang in LMS days.

One of the most attractive structures on the north side of Preston is the bridge carrying the main line over the Garstang-Claughton road. Badgers, the device of the Brockholes of Claughton Hall, appear on the stone cappings. Sadly, the bridge is better known as a road safety hazard than a work of architectural merit.

Much more famous are the Chorley "Flying Arches" on the south side of Preston. Constructed to hold back the sides of a cutting driven through difficult clay soil, they have needed virtually no maintenance since they were erected in 1843. The single course of stones at the centre is only 12 inches thick.

Part of the once complex layout at Kirkham North junction where the line from Preston divided for Lytham, Blackpool Central and Blackpool Talbot Road/Fleetwood. On the extreme right is the flyover taking the up line from Central over the Fleetwood tracks. The signal box was among the largest in Lancashire.

Poulton No.2 signal box with a down express passing a 2-4-2 tank. The Fleetwood and Blackpool lines diverge at the other end of the station.

Female company at the first signal box at Carleton, near Poulton, connected directly to the signalman's house. A 4-4-0 rushes over the level crossing.

The box was later replaced by another all-wooden structure, and the signalman's house demolished. This second box is in turn here being replaced by a brick-base cabin of L & NWR design (nearest the level crossing).

A line of cabs awaits passengers at Blackpool Talbot Road (later North). Note the exceptionally deep end screens to the roof of the station which, like all the Fylde lines, was jointly owned by the Lancashire & Yorkshire and London & North Western railways.

A busy street scene outside Talbot Road station about 1918. The horse is still the predominant form of transport, but a magnificent specimen of an early motor car as well as a tramcar are clearly visible.

"Luggage in Advance" was one of the hallmarks of a holiday in the railway age, and during the Lancashire Wakes weeks this could reach overwhelming proportions. Talbot Road station is almost lost in a sea of luggage in this view of about 1906.

Today railway traffic to Blackpool is greatly reduced, and the main portion of North (formerly Talbot Road) station has been closed. This new and much smaller station has been built on the site of the old excursion platforms.

The façade of Blackpool Central station about 1910. Lying at the end of the direct route from Preston, this was the most important of the resort's termini. Nevertheless, it was closed in 1964 and the site is now occupied by a bingo hall and car park.

Blackpool south shed, taken in the winter months about 1905 with 2-4-2 tank No. 84 outside the depot. During the summer an influx of up to 120 trains a day led to the shed being as congested as the pleasure beach!

A turn of the century view of Cleveleys station, which took its name from a coastal settlement two miles away! The station, on the Poulton-Fleetwood line, was later more sensibly named Thornton for Cleveleys.

In 1925 a new Thornton-Cleveleys station was built on the opposite side of the level crossing. This view shows the transition period with the new station completed but the old one not yet demolished.

A superb J. N. Tomlinson study of Lancashire & Yorkshire 4-4-2 No. 1423 leaving Poulton with a Manchester-bound excursion. The display of smoke would be for the special benefit of the photographer who had set up his camera at a pre-arranged location.

A curiosity was the Chief Mechanical Engineer's saloon of the Lancashire & Yorkshire Railway which had the tender and "carriage" on a single bogie underframe. Seen here at Fleetwood about 1910, it was used by George Hughes to travel throughout the system. The engine, 2-4-0 No. 731, was built by the L & NWR in 1878.

Fleetwood, a creation of the railway age, once saw steamers for the Isle of Man, Belfast, Whitehaven and Ardrossan (for Glasgow) sailing in connection with the trains. Those for the Isle of Man continued until 1961, using a landing stage seen in the process of demolition in the background of this 1964 photograph. Two years later the station was closed and has now been completely cleared.

The Fleetwood-Blackpool Talbot Road service was rendered ineffective by the tramcars following a more direct route between the two towns. Indicative of the lack of passengers is this rail-motor pausing at Wyre Dock station, which in 1966 became the terminus for Fleetwood.

An independent line which survived until Grouping, despite chronic shortage of funds, was the Garstang & Knott End Railway running through the sparsely populated northern Fylde. **Knott End** heads a train of transatlantic-style coaches at the terminus of the same name about 1911.

The 6½ mile Preston & Longridge Railway was opened as a horse-worked line in 1840, and ultimately became the joint property of the L & Y and L & NWR. The intermediate station of Grimsargh was photographed prior to the withdrawal of passenger services in 1930.

An interesting private railway was that to the County Mental Hospital, Whittingham, which left the Preston & Longridge at Grimsargh. Its two locomotives in 1951 were (left) 0-4-2 Barclay tank No. 1026 of 1904, and ex-London, Brighton & South Coast Railway 0-4-2 tank which was named **James Friar** on purchase in 1947.

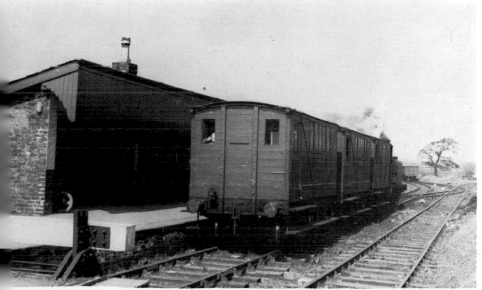

The passenger service on the hospital railway survived until closure in 1957, running in connection with buses following the withdrawal of Preston & Longridge trains. In this 1951 view at the railway's Grimsargh station, the rolling stock consists of converted brake vans.

Lancaster and Morecambe

Compared with much of the rest of Lancashire, the story of the railways of Lancaster and Morecambe is relatively straightforward. The first line into the town was the Lancaster & Preston Junction Railway, which opened its Greaves terminus in 1840. This was sited with the idea that the West Coast main line would continue northwards up the Lune Valley, but in fact the 1846 Lancaster & Carlisle Railway took a path through Carnforth and Oxenholme and a new through station had to be built at Lancaster Castle. The L & PJ had a bizarre existence, being leased for five years by the Lancaster Canal and then by the Lancaster & Carlisle, which in turn was leased by the London & North Western Railway in 1859 and absorbed by it 20 years later.

The North Western Railway, always known as the "little" North Western to distinguish it from the L & NW, completed its route from Skipton to a separate station at Lancaster Green Ayre in 1850. A connection to Castle created an indirect link between the West Riding and Scotland. The first portion of the "little" North Western had been opened in isolation in 1848 from Green Ayre to what up to then had been the small coastal settlement of Poulton. This took the name of Morecambe, the Harbour station being the embarkation point for steamer services to Piel (Barrow) and Belfast. Morecambe Town station was opened in

1851, and the "little" North Western leased by the Midland Railway in 1858 and absorbed by it 13 years later. Developments by this company at the turn of the century saw Town being replaced by Morecambe Promenade in 1907, and a line to the Midland's new port of Heysham Harbour being opened in 1904. In the meantime the Lancaster & Carlisle Railway had completed a branch from Hest Bank to Poulton Lane in 1864, a new terminus at Morecambe Euston Road being opened by the L & NW in 1886.

A less glamorous creation of the railway age in this area was Carnforth, initially served by the unimportant wayside station of Carnforth-Yealand on the Lancaster & Carlisle Railway. Its rise to importance began in 1857 when it became the junction for the Ulverston & Lancaster Railway, a line forming the main rail outlet from West Cumberland and Barrow to the south. It was absorbed in 1862 by the Furness Railway, which five years later completed a link from Carnforth to Wennington jointly with the Midland. This enabled Midland steamer services to be transferred from Morecambe to Piel where they remained until the opening of Heysham Harbour. The Furness and Midland had their own station at Carnforth until 1880 when a new station for the use of these companies and the L & NW was completed.

"Claughton" class 4-6-0 No. 695 **Sir Arthur Lawley** heads south from Lancaster Castle with a distinctly mixed bag of rolling stock. This is another scene which has been changed out of recognition with electrification of the West Coast route.

A much earlier electrification scheme was that of the Midland Railway between Lancaster Castle, Green Ayre, Morecambe Promenade and Heysham, inaugurated in 1908. A three-car unit awaits departure from Lancaster Castle in 1965, a year before the withdrawal of the service after it had been used for experiments in high-voltage 25kv electrification.

North Western expresses north of Lancaster. 4-6-0 "Prince of Wales" class no. 525 **Vulcan** eases its train through the cutting at Scotforth.

"Precursor tank" class 4-4-2T No. 2446 pounds past Hest Bank with an up local. The track on the left is the branch from Morecambe Euston Road.

Glasson Dock, one of the oldest ports on the west coast, was served by a branch from Lancaster Castle, completed in 1883 by the L & NWR at the instance of the Lancaster Port Commissioners. In this picture of about 1900 a Webb 0-6-0 tank is on the right. The branch was closed to passengers in 1930 and goods in 1964.

A view of the same period of Galgate, the first station south of Lancaster Castle on the main line. At this time it still had part of its original low-level platform and two separate waiting rooms.

Morecambe was another creation of the railway age, although it never quite managed to eclipse the popularity of Blackpool. Euston Road station, the terminus of the L & NWR branch into the town, was opened in 1886 and with its vivid yellow bricks must have looked almost indecent when new. This view dates from about 1919.

Bare Lane, the intermediate station on the L & NWR Morecambe branch, about 1918. Passengers waiting on its exposed platforms in a westerly gale have often thought the station well-named.

The Midland's Morecambe Promenade station replaced an earlier terminus in 1907. The light and spacious roof and the abundance of flower baskets give a gay atmosphere, although in fact this photograph was taken during the first world war.

Lancaster Green Ayre, on the main Midland route from the West Riding to Morecambe. Still retaining an attractive Midland signal gantry when photographed in 1958, it has since been completely demolished and the nearby rail crossing of the Lune utilised as a road bridge.

London & North Western tank engines. 0-6-2 tank No. 771 gives its crew adequate cab protection as it performs shunting duties at Lancaster Castle in 1902.

By contrast the driver of 0-6-0 tank No. 3210 shunting at Carnforth in the same year is fully exposed to the elements.

4-6-0 No. 45500 **Patriot,** the pioneer of its class, departs from Carnforth with an up express. The main line platforms here are now closed, the station remaining open only for trains to Barrow and Leeds.

An early study of Bolton-le-Sands station between Lancaster and Carnforth. Originally known just as Bolton, the "-le-Sands" was added to avoid confusion with the town in south Lancashire. Note the two signal arms on the single post.

The same station, still clearly recognisable in 1971. The signal box has gone and colour light signalling has appeared, but there is little to portend the vast change which was to come with electrification in 1974.

Hest Bank station looking towards Carnforth about 1900. At one time trains from the north for Morecambe arrived on the up platform (right), reversed on to the down line, came forward on to the branch (foreground), and then reversed into the bay platform before finally departing !

Hest Bank in 1971 after closure. The signal box has been replaced at the opposite end of the station, the down platform demolished and the junction with the branch moved north.

Acknowledgements

The photographs have been supplied by the following individuals and collections. Figures relate to page numbers; B=bottom; L=left; R=right; T=top:

J. B. Hodgson collection: 24B, 25T, 37B, 38T, 41, 49T, 50T, 51B, 53, 55T, 58T, 60T, 65R, 66T, 67, 68, 69T, 71T, 73T, 76, 77, 79T, 80, 81, 82, 83B.

John Marshall and collection: 17B, 18T, 22T, 29, 30TR, 37T, 46T, 54, 57, 61T, 63, 64, 65L, 75B, 83T, 87B.

Locomotive & General Railway Photographs: 9T, 16, 18B, 23T, 27T, 32B, 35, 42T, 48T, 74T, 84B, 88, 89, 95T.

David Joy: 33B, 40B, 46B, 49B, 59B, 60B, 61B, 66B, 69B, 79B, 91B.

H. C. Casserley and collection: 19, 20T, 21B, 31, 34T, 39B, 44T, 58B, 85.

B. Roberts and collection: 25B, 32T, 33T, 34B, 44B, 45B, 47T, 51T.

Real Photographs Co.: 20B, 27B, 30BR, 42B, 48B, 74B, 87T.

Eric Treacy: Front cover, 10, 11, 12, 13, 43, 72, 93.

Harold Bowtell and collection: 38B, 47B, 75T, 94B, 95B.

Sankey Collection: 40T, 78, 84T, 90, 91T.

W. A. Camwell: 17T, 24T, 30L, 55B.

Ken Nunn collection, Locomotive Club of Great Britain: 22B, 71B, 92.

British Railways: 73B, back cover.

Neville Fields collection: 39T, 45T.

Cox & Co. (Photographics) per Wilfred Spencer: 59T.

W. Crompton: 14, 15, 18.

T. A. Fletcher: 50B.

William Hulme (per Harold Bowtell): 21T.

E. Pouteau: 94T.

H. Townley collection: 56.

Arthur R. Wilson: 9B.

Miss M. H. Wolff (per Harold Bowtell): 23B.